VERMILION LEGACY

Also by Godhuli Chatterjee Gupta

Desert Marigold

VERMILION LEGACY

POEMS BY

GODHULI CHATTERJEE GUPTA

Vermilion Legacy

ISBN: 979-8-234-03621-6

Cover art - *Kumartuli (Clay Goddess)* by Pothik Chatterjee.
Edited by Freydis Lova.
Cover layout by Rachel Clift.
Book design & layout by Rachel Clift.
rcliftpoetry.com

First printing edition, 2026.

wordsbygodhuli.com
@wordsby.godhuli
Godhuli Chatterjee Gupta

For all the women who came before us

"I go forth along, and stand as ten thousand."

— Maya Angelou, *Our Grandmothers*

VERMILION

noun
ver • mil • ion

1 : a vivid reddish orange
2 : a bright red pigment consisting of mercuric sulfide
broadly : any various red pigments

3 : sindoor, a bright red powder applied to a woman's hair parting by her husband on her wedding day in South Asian cultures, marking a significant transition from woman to bride
4 : an energetic red, representing auspiciousness and good fortune
5 : a vibrant red hue signifying female energy, vitality, and passion
6 : the color of our beating heart, our soul, the soil of our beloved motherland

TABLE OF CONTENTS

INTRODUCTION

This is a project that has been *burning* inside me for many years, even before I picked up a pen to start writing poetry. I remember having dinner with one of my oldest friends over ten years ago, both of us tearing up as we spoke about our Indian mothers who packed up their bags to marry strangers, crossing international borders to start new lives and families with virtually no emotional or physical support system. *How did they do it?* we both thought out loud, incredulously. In my mother's case, this meant starting anew every three to four years in a new country or continent, as my father was an engineer working for a multinational oil company that transferred him to a new role every few years. She was perpetually on a spousal visa, with no legal work opportunities beyond the walls of our new company-sanctioned apartment or house, which she swiftly converted into a gorgeous sanctuary that always felt like home within the first few weeks of our new moves. Whether we were in Paris, Abu Dhabi, Jakarta, Houston, or Mumbai, my brother and I always felt right at home thanks to my mother's magical ability to create roots regardless of geographic location.

My mother's story is not uncommon, but that does not make it any less remarkable. Our immigrant mothers and grandmothers each have extraordinary tales to tell—stories of fleeing politically unstable countries as refugees, starting over in foreign lands, learning new languages, developing new professional skills, building careers, persevering in the midst of adversity over and over again, all while devoting their entire lives to the health and happiness of their children. Ten years ago, I vowed to create something that would honor and acknowledge their tremendous sacrifices and tell the stories that have been drowned out in history. As a mother myself today, I am so acutely aware of the immense transformations our mothers must have experienced being stripped of everything they knew to build a new life of their own. Beyond the pain and immense loss, there is a deep well of ancestral strength and exuberant joy that stems from this generation of immigrant women that I want to highlight as well. During a time when immigrants are under attack across the globe, it is time we celebrate and acknowledge their enduring resilience. Their capacity to love, provide, and thrive against all odds is inspiring, and I hope it empowers future generations in their own paths of unique self-discovery.

I had the pleasure of not only mining my own ancestral history, but speaking to other South Asian women about their immigrant experiences as well. I was struck by the grit and radical acts of resistance demonstrated by our mothers and grandmothers. These conversations challenged the notion that immigrant women from prior generations are only defined by their ability to silently tolerate pain and hardship. They resisted and pushed through challenges in their own unique and defiant acts of rebellion, a quality certainly inherited by the sons and daughters of immigrants. I am deeply grateful to everyone who spoke to me— your stories matter and I refuse to let them be erased in our history. While my focus here is on the experience of South Asian immigrant women, I believe these stories will resonate universally as they touch on global themes of identity, connection, displacement, and perseverance.

So here it is— my deeply personal way of thanking my mother, my grandmothers, and all the women who came before us for their lineage of love and courage that drives me everyday. A collection of poems that honor their stories, their pain, their grief, their power and their joy. May we learn to forgive, to break cycles, and to let the breadth of their experiences become a source of strength and motivation for us to keep going. And to keep spreading love.

Thank you will never be enough.

Godhuli Chatterjee Gupta

JOURNEY

The First to Begin a Life Anew

"For being a foreigner, Ashima is beginning to realize, is a sort of lifelong pregnancy—a perpetual wait, a constant burden, a continuous feeling out of sorts."

— Jhumpa Lahiri, *The Namesake*

Matrimony

Here is a girl with a passion for philosophy,
skin glowing with milk-white purity,
her hips too *slender*
for fertility.

Here is a girl with a penchant for the arts,
voice woven with silk & honey, but
her midnight complexion a few shades
deeper than we please.

Here is a girl— all such lovely girls, but some
too tall, *too* proud, *too* hungry, *too* loud.

How will we betroth and parade
such a girl? Who keeps her gaze
steadily towards the sun, even as
the whole world says *no*.

An Unwilling Betrayal

It was you, Ma,
who spun the fragile thread
of my childhood, delicately
weaving the tapestry of
our shared dreams.

It was you, Ma,
who taught me to use my voice,
to pursue excellence, to demand
justice when it was *nowhere*
to be found.

It was you, Ma,
who created every fiber
of my being & infused my
vessels with a river of love
that almost *suffocated* me.

Why is it then,
that your sons were bestowed with
with titles, accolades & glittering palaces?
And your daughters, gifted away
to *foreign lands*?

Why is it that you gave
the most precious slivers
of your soul away to him,
or is it maybe—

that you had no choice at all?

Wolf Pack

When the world desired
only sons from her womb,
she stood tall and birthed
daughters instead.

She armed them with booming
voices, an unshakeable resilience,
the inability to look away
from unspeakable injustices.

When they would all ask,
what is a life with only daughters?
She would laugh, proudly calling
them her *wolf pack.*

They were sisters bound
for eternity, their mother's courage
flowing like molten gold through
intertwining veins.

A life without my daughters,
she would whisper to herself,
is a life *unlived.*

A Life Anew

The photo still exists
somewhere in a forgotten album,
the edges curled up,
little speckles splayed upon
the black & white faces,
as if the weight of grief
in their eyes was too much
for the world to bear.

But you can still see the brave
painted smiles of a mother,
a father, brothers, and sisters
as they bid farewell to their
eldest married daughter,
the first to begin a life anew
with a man she barely *knew*.

Foreign Tongues

Don't you think it's a bit silly
to point and laugh at foreign tongues?
When you are the one missing the
sheer *poetry* in words from worlds apart.

The ebbs and flows in a single phrase,
the melodies floating from thoughts
exchanged, the complexities and
hidden treasures from oceans away,
breathing *history* into our mouths.

Village

Where is the village
she was promised?

The village she was once
so intrinsically a part of,
the sound of bellowing laughter & trivial banter,
the familiar warmth of aunts & cousins & babies
all carrying each other through the
tiring tediousness of their days.

Where are they now?

The silence is deafening,
the solitude swallows her,
the baby's cries cut through
the air like a jolt of venom
piercing through her skin.

She looks around at the
emptiness and knows that the
village must rise within her,
in the vastness of her love,
in the strength of her surrender,
and in her capacity to *survive*.

Only as She Knows

I love watching my friends
become *mothers*.

I love watching this new ethereal
version of her unfolding in front
of my eyes, even when she may
not see the beauty of her own
magical *metamorphosis*.

Does she know how beautiful
she looks as she soothes her crying
child, in all her raw and radiant
vulnerability? How the soft contour
of her body melts into the delicate
rolls of her little miracle?

I am desperate to let her know
all of this—that even as her heart
aches & agonizes & dissects every
decision she makes, she has already
transformed into the most exquisite
being, resplendent and rooted in
her deep, ancestral knowing.

The only one to mother hers,
only *as she knows*.

Evening Prayers

Every evening before the world
slowly darkens, she excuses herself
from the doldrum of her duties
to offer evening prayers in solitude
to the deities who protect her soul.

She collects the petals from her
morning foraging, of jasmine and
marigold and hibiscus, gathering
them in the delicate folds of her
simple cotton sari[1].

She sprinkles her modest temple
with the vibrant colors of her
boundless devotion, a simple act
of her gratitude, self-love,
and self-preservation.

She blows her conch shell,
its powerful echo reverberating
through her home, splitting her
heart wide open with joy and serenity
as *Ma Durga*[2] smiles down on her.

Her children smile too,
knowing exactly where their Ma is,
as she marks the end of yet
another day.

[1] a large, unstitched piece of fabric traditionally worn by South Asian women, draped intricately over their bodies
[2] the protective mother goddess of the universe and one of the principal forms of Shakti, the divine female energy

Winter in America

First comes the indescribable magic
of your first winter snowfall—
soft balls of powdery cotton floating
from the heavens, covering the ground
in a shimmering carpet of glitter.

Then comes the deep, biting frost
that settles inside your bones, as you
desperately layer your body in
scarves & blankets over saris,
thick socks under sneakers.

You eventually buy the discounted
winter coat from a church in the nice
neighborhood, but even that cannot
lift your spirits from not seeing
the sun in what feels like eternity.

It's beautiful here, you write
in letters to your relatives, glorifying
the cleanliness, the quiet, when in
reality you feel like you are drowning
in the solitude of a long winter.

When all you desire is
the *dust & chaos & warmth*
of *home*.

Arrival of Spring

Perhaps the greatest gift
of a long winter is the sheer
joy and intoxication we feel at the
arrival of spring as she unfurls
her shimmering fingers to
welcome us into her arms.

I give in to her radiant
embrace, allowing her to
awaken what's been resting
within me, to rejoice in the
sudden vibrations that begin
to hum in my soul.

This rhythm of life,
it goes *on and on*, yet
the profound simple truth
that the *light will always come*,
still leaves me in wonder
and awe at the sheer
miracle of it all.

Labor

In the assembly lines of factories / operating rooms /
community colleges / special education classrooms /
libraries / laboratories / volunteering organizations /
PTAs / motels / restaurants / community gatherings /
gas stations / religious institutions / banks /
boardrooms / corporate cubicles / courtrooms /
local stores / spice-laced kitchens, meticulously
preserving ancestral recipes / daycares / art studios /
the hallways of her own home / her child's bedroom,
wiping away tears and imparting lessons of wisdom /
inside the hearts of the next generation.

They all found a way to labor,
to keep rising against the grain,
to keep building futures
brick by brick,
pouring *grit*
into our souls.

I Know We'll be Okay

There are so many *nos* in our day,
so many moments of little poisons.
No, you may not eat that, play with that,
wear that, act like that.

Even I become frightened by
the acidity in my tongue, the daggers
in my words, a guttural punch
to my soul.

Am I passing down a lineage
of rage? An obsession with trying
to mold a vibrant wildflower into
a synthetic rose?

Then I hold you close to my chest,
and I see how much you need me
to say, *I'm sorry*, that, *I love you*
as you are.

So I do, over and over again.
and I know we'll be okay
in this moment of forgiveness,
in this moment of *only love.*

Fragments

When your soul belongs to different homes,
you feel like you exist in fragments.
Like there is always something deeply innate
missing from your core, gently coaxing
you towards a different shore.

It is a heavy burden to encompass
so many people & places in your heart.
To see the ashes of your identity swirl from
east to west, and to wonder what it would
feel like to keep it all in one place.

But oh, *what a gift*, as well.
To collect the dazzling little slivers
of your soul and wear them like
the gorgeous accessories they are.
To walk, to sway, to talk

with an entire galaxy in your breath.

The Wound of Loss

This too, can be a family's
inheritance— the wound of loss.
A *mastery* of bidding farewell
over & over again to everything
that once belonged to their hearts.

A child leaves her ancestral village in
present-day Bangladesh, to seek refuge
in the chaos of post-colonial Kolkata.
A young bride leaves modern India
to seek prosperity in the Middle East
as the wife of an expatriate. Her children
leave their lives as worldly citizens to
pursue education, career, and love
in the United States.

Where will *their* children go next?
Will they always be in search
of something better, hearts shattered
in a million different people & places?
What is the meaning of these borders,
these labels, these identities,
if they will always be torn away?

What is a world that cannot keep us safe?

Takat

Takat[3] is the flame within me
that refuses to be extinguished.
Takat is the steady grip of my
soul's true yearning, infusing me
with softness & might.
If only you could see the embers
that smolder silently beneath
the surface. If only you knew
the *takat* it takes to keep breathing
fire into the next generation,
to ignite the flames of their desires,
to make them believe it will
all be better.

To *insist* that they must try.

[3] strength in Hindu and Urdu

Veena[4]

How could I ever feel alone
when I have the infinite, patient
& sacrificial love of music
always by my side?

Waiting patiently in the silent corridors
of my life, greeting me with joy and without
an ounce of pride or resentment when I am
ready to be re-acquainted with the divine
strings of *Saraswati*[5] incarnate.

I hold my *Veena's* soft curves in my arms
like a long-lost lover, floating through land
after land of Vedic scriptures and temple
carvings, picking up pieces of myself
I thought I had lost along the way.

I am captivated by the divine melodies
that emerge effortlessly from my fingers,
a prisoner to the heavenly harmonies
created by this instrument of otherworldly
purity and indescribable beauty.

What a gift to have this *love*,
to find myself again in your
ever-present, tender embrace.

[4] a traditional, plucked string instrument used in Indian music
[5] the Goddess of arts, wisdom, music, writing and learning

Aunties

When she couldn't watch her
own baby, she would frantically knock
on her neighbor's doors, eyes pleading
for a quick favor.

Whether it was *Sanjana* or *Aditi* or
Farzana Aunty, they would always
open the door with a reassuring smile,
taking the baby in their loving arms,
their homes always smelling like a
sanctuary of laughter and spices.

I don't mind when I see them today,
as they pinch my cheeks & have
something to say about the way I look.
I don't mind at all, when I know
how they always saved the day.

How they were always there,
for a mother yearning
for someone to *care*.

Female Kinship

Sometimes you just need
the softness & divine energy
alignment of another woman.
To feel their presence, their
tender touch, the camaraderie
of your shared pain and
collective joy.

To have someone hold
your emotions in the palm
of their hands and tell you
they're beautiful and not
a *burden*.

She

She pours herself a cup of tea, standing by
the kitchen window, allowing herself to be
swathed by the gentle autumn light.

She welcomes the tranquility, the luxury
of stillness, even as she mourns the euphoric chaos
of muddy feet & sticky arms around her waist.

The sadness comes in crackling waves, the relief
in guilty ripples. But isn't this it, the magic of *being*?
To know it all *moves on*—

Just as the sun is swallowed up by the celestial
dust, the gliding geese surrender to the whispering
wind. At least she was there to see it.

To immerse herself in *joy*.

RESONANCE

Her Touch Carried With Her

"How can I leave this world without leaving her my spirit? So this is what I will do. "

— Amy Tan, *The Joy Luck Club*

Sacrifices

To all the mothers
and grandmothers whose
sacrifices we praise,
instead of shedding light
on the oppression of the
men who silenced you—
we're sorry for the ways
we failed you.

For never giving you
the chance to say *no*.

An Ode to My Grandmother

This is an ode to my grandmother—
who possessed very little but the petals
plucked from her garden every morning,
humming prayers for those around her.

This is an ode to my grandmother—
a widow far too young, sacrificing color from
her wardrobe for the apples of her grandchildren's
cheeks & the diamonds in their eyes.

This is an ode to my grandmother—
stripped so suddenly of societal rights,
powerless in her voice,
petite in her stature.

But her touch, *oh her touch*—
how it overflowed with grace & compassion,
and that indomitable sense
of *knowing*.

Her touch carried with her
an ocean of love, pouring courage
into those she held, bursting with
power beyond measure.

Kahani[6]

When we were little kids spending
summers in India, we used to love curling up
with our grandmother, begging her to share
stories from her childhood across the border.
We were so curious, so ravenous for her words
as we buried ourselves deep into her *kahanis*,
mesmerized by every magical little detail
from her bank of broken memories.

Then, one year, we stopped asking.
We buried ourselves in books, films,
and our own trivial little lives. And
I still wonder sometimes, how often she
must have longed for us to ask her for just

one more kahani.

[6] *story, tale, or narrative* in Hindi and Urdu

Monsoon Summers in Calcutta

I remember so vividly—
the soul crushing humidity,
the deep tremor of torrential downpour
and clapping thunder, the unsettling discomfort
of moisture under my feet when entering bathrooms,
the crippling boredom of life without technology,
the anger & resentment towards my parents
for summers so mundane & unglamorous.

But what I remember the most
are the lines on my grandmother's
frail hands and her gentle embrace
as she caressed my face and asked
when we would be back again.

Ancestry

When you think of the word
ancestry, you may think of all the
symbols deeply intertwined
with the fists of patriarchy—
the trickling down of names,
estates, rigid traditions,
and certain decorums.

But when I think of ancestry,
I think of the matriarchs who breathed
fire into my chest, the intricate recipes
that nourished me, the sacred blessings
that protected me, the unyielding love
that formed the understory
of my every glory.

How then, are their voices
so easily erased from the
records of our history?
How is it not *their* names
that are boasted about
in our stories?

Names Like Poems

Niharika. Fatima. Geeta.
Jamila. Mina. Elizabeth.
Laila. Safiya. Rani. Lila.
Arundhati. Kalpana.
Zainab. Nargis. Krishna.
Mary. Shanti. Vrinda.

With names that sound like
poems humming in our souls,
may we say them out loud
so they echo throughout history.

Like the blessings from which
they came from,
like the *fire* from
which they rose.

You Somehow Made a Home

With only a few jars of spices,
a sack of old rice,
your loving hands folding
melted butter with steaming
bhaat[7] and boiled eggs,
you somehow made
a home.

[7] *rice* in Bengali

The Phone Call

One of the sharpest, most
excruciating memories from my
childhood, that still cuts me like a dagger,
was waking up to the guttural wails
from my mother or grandmother
as they received the phone call
from back home that they
never wanted to receive.

One of their own was no more.

There is no time to mourn,
no time to bid farewell,
there is simply *no time.*
In between the frantic
arrangements to fly back home,
in between the thick fog of guilt
and regret of not being physically
next to the person who was
once part of your soul.

How does one mourn a death
a thousand miles away?
How does one begin to *forgive*
themselves for choosing a life away?

How do you continue to exist
with the suffocating pain
and longing to be here, there,
everywhere?

Ma's Closet

My mother's closet overflows with
gorgeous threads inherited from the
queens of our lineage—luscious silk,
velvet and chiffon, all kissed by
generations of history & heritage.

Can you smell the delicate notes
of pashmina & sandalwood? Can you
feel the pride & sweat of the artisans
who painstakingly etched each intricate
thread, the *layers* of magic & folk?

Try as you may to turn our woven
legacy into polyester profits stripped
of our vibrant pasts & rich identities,
you cannot erase the souls from
which we rose. You cannot swallow
the voice of a *queen*.

Don't Lose Your Fingerprints

I once watched my mother press
the crumbling ridges of her callused fingers
on an ink pad, then a scanner, the color
draining from her face as she realized
her fingerprints were *nowhere* to be found.

The same hands that once caressed me
as a child, soothed my fears, washed dishes,
cooked *endlessly* had somehow lost the
intricate mazes and magical mosaics
that belonged only to *her*.

What happens when the very thing
that is meant to uniquely define you
is wiped away? Who are you beneath
the vibrant colors, the burning spices,
the fading *mehndi*?[8]

We adorn our hands with henna
& bangles when perhaps we should
marvel at the beauty that already
exists within. Celebrate the fragile
fabric of our identities.

To never forget all that makes us
extraordinary.

[8] beautiful, intricate designs painted on the skin using henna paste

Packing List

Do girls wear shorts in India now?
I ask my mother on the phone
as I decide what sort of role
I will play on my first trip back
to the motherland since becoming
a mother.

I've played it all before—
demure hometown girl,
urban expat in Mumbai,
the foreign daughter
in foreign clothes
drawing curious stares
on the streets of Calcutta.

The thing is,
I'm not even sure what clothes
will suit me now. If this land
even has a place for a woman torn
between jeans & *churidars*[9].
A woman who simply wants
to come as she is.

Naked and begging
to *belong*.

[9] Indian trousers, tight around the ankles, typically worn with a longer tunic

Never Lost in Translation

Maybe you don't *need* to know
the same language, I realize a few days
into my children's first trip to India.
I fight back tears as I watch them jump right
into the irresistible chaos of my land, absorbing
their surroundings with wide eyes & open hearts.
What a beautiful thing it is to watch them
take their great aunties' frail hands into theirs.
To witness the joy their little smiles bring to
the people who have been counting down
the days and years to meet them.
To watch them dance and rejoice with cousins,
and to realize that maybe, some things
were never meant to be lost in translation.

A touch, a smile, a hug can somehow
feel *enough*.

Taste of My Motherland

I close my eyes and I can still taste,
feel, smell the dizzying, intoxicating
madness of my motherland.

The sticky residue of a slow monsoon morning
seeping into every particle of my body.
The suffocating humidity reverberating off my skin.
The taste of *mughlai* chicken rolls[10] from alleyways
of Gariahat[11]. The cacophony of sounds at
every street turn. The warmth of large family
gatherings at cobweb-filled ancestral homes,
with sari-clad aunties serving platter after platter
of syrupy-drenched sweets. The hours spent
sweating in a black & yellow *Ambassadors*[12]
en route to what seemed like nowhere, smiling
and reluctantly accepting hugs from long-lost
relatives who have no reason to love you
beyond shared names & the goodwill of our
elders. And yet somehow they still do, so *deeply*
and unconditionally.

I close my eyes and worry I will forget,
for it has been too long since I have felt
the taste of my motherland in my mouth.

[10] a popular street food, blending Indian, Persian, and Central Asian flavors
[11] a vibrant shopping neighborhood in the city of Kolkata (previously known as Calcutta)
[12] the name of Kolkata's iconic bright yellow taxis

Gold

When I adorned myself in heirloom
gold jewels as a rapturous young bride,
it wasn't because I loved the aesthetic
of gold layered on gold, or because I
wanted to make a style statement for the
wedding magazines of our generation.

I wore them because those jewels
carried with them the blessings & patina
of the matriarchs who came
before me, passed down by
my mother, my aunts, my
grandmothers, my great-aunts.

Those jewels rooted them in
financial certainty when they had none.
A symbol of their power, their style,
their timeless elegance. Their ability
to stand tall as the queens that
they deserved to be.

A kiss from the heavens,
a kiss from my grandmothers.
When they couldn't be there
to see me walking around fire,
I could still feel their gentle embrace
and spirit wrapped around me
in infinite blessings.

To let me know that
they were there,
they were there.

They are always *here*.

Carry Within Me

What is it about our grandmothers
that their spirit stays deep within you
long after their souls have departed?

What is it about their tender softness,
paired with a brutal, impenetrable
strength that somehow seems to guide
you from the heavens on this manic,
twisting river of our lives?

Oh, what a *blessing*, to be engulfed
in the wildest tempest of her prayers.
To carry on a sliver of her impossible
legacy, forever shielded by her
love and devotion.

The love that I will always
carry within me, in the deepest
crevices of my *being*.

The Silhouette

I close my eyes and can still remember the peace,
stability, and infinite joy you worked tirelessly
to infuse into our childhood, even when your
own world felt like chaos at times.

I still remember how *beautiful* you made us feel,
treating us like your divine little Lakshmis[13],
teaching us that self-love and self-care
can be a worthy endeavor.

I still remember how you stood by my side
as I trudged through the early days of motherhood,
soothing me, nurturing me, empowering me
to rise above the haziness of it all.

How you manifested the dreams you didn't
dare dream for yourself, your eyes sparkling as
you adorned us with *ghungroos*[14] & ancestral jewels,
clapping proudly as we twirled on stage.

None of this must have been easy— to mother
with such rigor and devotion, infusing your
trademark humor and grit even in the most
turbulent moments of our becoming.

All I dream for us now is to
share the burden of your endless love.
To let me carry the torch you've burned
so brightly for us.

Do you see the silhouette of us
walking together, arm in arm?
Blessed by the love of the matriarchs
who marched ahead of us,

Fingers outstretched
toward the horizon,
so hopeful & bright.

[13] the Goddess of wealth, fortune, beauty, and prosperity
[14] a set of small, metallic bells worn as an anklet for Indian classical dance performances

Pretty

Our mothers wanted us to be pretty,
scrubbing our bodies down from head
to toe with bleach and homemade
beauty elixirs of *besan*[15] & honey.

Our mothers wanted us to be pretty,
reminding us to put on eyeliner
or to wear the dress that showed
off our suffocated figures.

Our mothers wanted us to be pretty,
because it was the only way they knew
how to protect us from a world that held
doors wide open for *pretty little fools*.

What a gift it is now to call my
daughter smart, and funny, and
brazenly independent. To know
she can carve her own path
and kick doors wide open

without the burden
of *pretty*.

[15] *chickpea flour* in Hindi, traditionally used in Indian skincare for exfoliation and brightening

Mothers & Daughters

I watch my mother soften
& transform into the same ethereal
being my grandmother once was.
I watch her laugh & chase my gleeful
daughter around the house,

Calling her *beautiful,*
perfect & intelligent.

I choose to wrap myself up
in this moment of bliss, in this
moment of tenderness.
I choose to let her words
& affection pour through
my daughter and into me.

I allow myself to feel her
love flowing through our veins,
bottling it up for generation
after generation.

I allow myself to heal.
For here, now & *eternity*.

Dear Ma

Sometimes the words *I love you* or *thank you*
sit heavily like sharp stones on our tongues,
like the weight of those words is simply too much
to bear, too unceremonious for the one who is so
deeply ingrained in the fabric of my being.

For the one who brought me into this world,
held me through my fears, and continues
to offer a steady hand as we make our way into
the great unknown. Sometimes it feels impossible
to show my gratitude to a life's devotion.

No words can do justice.
No acts can adequately portray.

But still I need you to know that my heart
collects and keeps every little thing you do.
From the morning texts to the platters
of my current cravings, to the way you fuss
over my health, while compromising your own
as you chase after my children.

To your unwavering strength in the midst
of my chaos and all of life's uncertainties,
offering the intangible layers of support
remiss from your own early years of mothering.

And just as we feel our ancestors with every
step and every breath, I hope you can feel
the way your love flows through me for eternity.
immortalized for generations to come,
igniting the steady flame.

LEGACY

The Grand Crescendo

"Even when I'm long gone, you carry my name. Never forget: I am with you always."

— Abraham Verghese, *The Covenant of Water*

Cosmic Song

Whether you exist in this universe
or another, perhaps a different time,
a different generation, a different era—
your soul will always know the melody
of its cosmic song.

Your body rose, after all,
from the light of lotus petals,
your eyes quiver with the fire
of a million desert suns,
and your dewy melanin glistens
with the ashes of your ancestors
whose steps will always echo
within you.

Try as they may to break the thread
that binds you to your origins,
to erase the markers that make you
uniquely divine, your soul
will *always* find a way.

To hear the whispers of those
who came before you, to listen
carefully to its lore of creation.

To never stop dancing
to the rhythm of its
cosmic song.

Things That Are Brown and Beautiful

The rich soil beneath our feet,
laying the foundation for new life.
The soft clay tenderly sculpted by artisans
into goddesses & exquisite little statues.
The luscious woodwork of historic homes,
keeper of ancient whispers & legacies.
The Ganga river in her most powerful form—
swirling & cascading & blessing her way
through bustling cities and towns.
Glossy new leather that smells like
a rainy escape deep into the woods.
Burnt caramel oozing of sugary
sweetness and divine complexity.
A velvety smooth cup of your
morning coffee, leaving tiny drops
on your lover's mouth.

The color of his skin.
The color of my skin.
The undeniably exquisite
colors of our skin.

Jagged

These days I find myself embracing
the jagged edges of my soul a little more.
Feeding little morsels of fuel to the parts
of myself that can no longer be quelled.

I summon my inner Kali[16], granting her
free will to flaunt her rage & righteousness.
I give her permission to stand tall, speak
her mind, emit brilliance wherever she goes.

You see, we were never meant to be
porcelain statues, flawless & lifeless.
We were built to be complicated, uneven,
perhaps even a little bit broken.

We were made to flow, to transcend,
to evolve. To simply be

human.

[16] the Goddess of power, time, destruction, and fertility.

Generational

We hear so often about
generational trauma, the unknowing
wounds bequeathed by our ancestors
that rock our core to this very day.

But what about the generational gifts—
the acts of kindness, resilience and
community ingrained into the very
essence of our beings?

The way our mothers invited strangers
into our homes for chai & samosas[17],
simply because they were connected
by a distant friend or a shared name.

The way we still reach out to another
with the same skin & shared history,
craving a connection bridging our ancestral
ties & our lonely modern existence.

The way our ache for
community remains so strong
across oceans & generations.
The way we still persist,
even when our scars try
to bring us down.

[17] a fried Indian savory pastry, stuffed with spiced meat or vegetables

To Honor Her Legacy

You must
~~Be ambitious~~
~~Break free of everyone's expectations~~
~~Never give up~~
~~Be kind~~
~~Be empathetic~~
~~Be tenacious~~
~~Be the voice they never had~~
~~Fight back against the patriarchy~~
~~Revel in your freedom~~
~~Stand up for everyone else~~
~~Be empowered to make your own decisions~~
~~Be successful~~
~~Climb the corporate ladder~~
~~Take care of your family~~
~~Live a life of service~~
~~Break free of toxicity~~
~~Seek a respectable partner~~
~~Take control of your own life~~
Simply be who you are meant to be.

Just a Girl

As I watch my mother today,
I yearn for her to dream
without anchors. I wish to unravel
all her inhibitions thread by thread,
for her to tell me with authority
what she *really* wants, how she
would like to spend her days,
to not feel like her world is simply
an orbit around mine.

I hope she knows that she can
be reckless, selfish, and spontaneous,
to make up for all the times that
she could not.

That I will love her even so.
That she is worthy
as she is.

Revolution

Your battles may not look like
Goddess Durga's triumphant march
as she tramples & slays the buffalo demon,
or like Rani of Jhansi's[18] majestic entrance
into war as she swings her sword
with the weight of her child
strapped to her back.

Yours feels quieter,
less visible,
less acknowledged,
less *victorious*.

But never forget, yours is still
the journey of a goddess in constant
motion. One with the spirit
and ravenous fury of a warrior
queen with raging lions
in her heart.

Never once giving up
on her quiet *revolution*.

[18] a legendary warrior queen in the Indian Rebellion of 1857 against the British East Indian Company

Limitless

Why hesitate in sharing your love,
why be timid in the way you touch?
Be indulgent, unrestrained,
excessive in the way you wrap
your entire being around the
people you love.

We are all made of the same
cosmic dust, brimming with
infinite emotions & a yearning
for connection. Think of the magic
that could radiate when love is
met with only more love.

When love is *limitless*.

Look at You

Look at you,
dancing your way through life,
proudly wearing the blessings of your ancestors,
celebrating your culture with exuberant joy,
flaunting the gorgeous ethnic threads
that adorn your beautiful melanin
glistening in the sun.

You never knew you could,
but here you are standing tall
and embracing everything
that makes you *you*.

Boasting the many layers
of your multifaceted identity
& basking in its divine fluidity.
You never knew you could,
but you walked through fire
and came out burning

an *inextinguishable* flame.

To Be a Woman Today

Is to be ripped apart in headlines,
on the streets, in the lyrics of your
favorite rap song, your every *move*
scrutinized under a telescope, like
a pawn swerved between two extremes.

You're either a man-eater or a
#tradwife, childbearing or miserable,
demonized or glorified, worshiped
on media's altar or canceled, no room
left for nuance or complexity.

And yet, what a *gift*.

What an indescribable magic,
this unbreakable spirit. To keep
fighting for our voice, for our worth,
to keep reaching for one another
to join hands and say *we want more.*

To keep going.
To keep going.
To keep going.

All The Women Who Came Before Us

Every night when I look into
my daughter's eyes, I see a mosaic
of all the women who came before us—
her grandmother's piercing stare,
brimming with love and intensity,
her aunt's luscious tresses commanding
the attention of a lioness, her mother's
fragile, yet tender beating heart, and
the fiery *passion* that binds us all.

What a gift to watch her discover
all the generational magic that
already exists deep within her.
What a gift to watch her unravel
the old from the new, concocting
her own beautiful elixir as she
lights her way down an unpaved
path, her soul singing with the
resounding cheer & blessings

of all the women who came before us.

Masterpiece

There are times I feel her presence
the most. In the early rays of morning
light, I imagine holding her gaze as
she crystallizes before me.

A luscious temple of shadows
and complexities. Her terracotta
foundation built with love by her
ancestry, but every layer, color
& curve curated with care by
no one else but me.

I step into her embrace,
melting away the inner sorrows
and battle wounds discovering
both tenderness & fire.

And just as the marigold finds her
way towards the sun, I can see with a
renewed *drasti*[19], the resplendent shine
of my masterpiece—

The woman I was always meant to be.

[19] gaze, sight, or viewpoint in Sanskrit

Little Empires

I once tiptoed through this world
in timid little whispers, checking off
arbitrary boxes of someone else's
monochromatic dreams until
it was someone else's turn
to watch and learn
from my every move.

Perhaps my greatest legacy now
is to *glide* through this world
with unapologetic audacity,
unmoored by society's pull,
doggedly persistent in chasing
my own rapture.

If for nothing else, but to show you
that your own path to ambition
is enough. That the only victory
worth chasing is your own bliss.

That little *empires* can be created
from your happiness alone.

Crescendo

I used to think I could be
the conductor of your life's
composition, until you taught
me to let go & watch your own
divine rhythm unfold.

I used to think I could be
your sculptor, shaping my own
beautiful piece of clay, until you
stretched & wiggled your long limbs
out of my arms & into this world.

It's hard to explain this dichotomy
of blistering joy and wistful pain.
How I want to hold onto the softness
& naivety of your youth, even as you
begin to rise tall on your own.

Try as I may to conduct & to sculpt,
I know now my purpose is to sit proudly
in your ensemble. To stay in sync with
your flow, to honor the melody in your
soul, and to stand by you in awe,

as you make your way to
the grand *crescendo*.

Good Girls, Part II[20]

I watch my daughter
cartwheel in public,
dance without inhibition
while swaying her hips
& hugging everyone around her,
firmly declining when
she's not in the mood.

I watch my daughter
say *no* with utmost defiance,
rattling off all her dreams
with unabashed confidence,
her eyes on fire
with zany glee.

Good girl, good girl,
I think to myself.
Go show them
just how *good*
you can be.

[20] The poem "Good Girls" is from Godhuli Chatterjee Gupta's inaugural poetry collection *Desert Marigold*

More Than Aesthetics

If only you knew
the low, slicked-back buns of your childhood
would become the *aesthetic* of choice,
the gleaming gold jewels your mother
set aside for your wedding day
would grace music festivals,
the herbal remedies of your ancestors
would become *their* wellness secret,
& the textiles of your motherland's
markets would grace
everyone's home.

If only you knew
to wear it all with pride
so they can see the *depth*
of our roots, before they cut
off the stems, and only show
what blooms above.

To the Culture Makers

To the culture makers,
the carriers of ancient
traditions, the stewards
of our ancestral wisdom.

I see the way you navigate
the dichotomy within you,
swirling your very own melting pot
of identities to collect & keep
what your heart desires.

I see you working tirelessly to fuse
those jewels onto the next generation—
walking into classrooms with diyas[21]
& rangolis[22], while adorning your
home with marigolds and ghouls.

I see you planting the seeds
of our culture, giving your
children *permission* to embrace
the richness of their roots,
to wear it with radiance.

And above all,
the permission to choose
themselves in all their
joyful *abundance*.

[21] small oil lamps made of clay, typically used during Diwali, the festival of lights, to light candles and decorate the home
[22] intricate, traditional floor art that women in India use to decorate their entryways during the festive season of Diwali

When Society Says, *No*

Stand by your convictions.
Draw your line in the sand.

Recognize that for the rest of your life
the pessimists, the naysayers, your very
own self-doubt will try their best to make
mayhem of your volition. To erase your
persuasion. Keep holding your head high
and *draw that line*. Even when you don't feel
it, you must dig your claws into the compass
of your soul and find its direction.

To honor the immovable truth
within you will be the greatest
victory of them all.

Kali

Bless her simmering rage,
her boundless freedom, her
audacity to exist as *herself*
in a world that idolizes only
the demure & the virtuous.

Allow her river of fire to
flow through your tongue,
and bathe yourself in the
magnificent aura that bows
down to no one but *herself*.

Do you see how good it feels?
To uncloak yourself from
performance & adoration.
To simply *exist* in all our
divine, naked glory.

Let Us

Let us rest,
because they could not.

Let us wear our emotions
with the vulnerability and pain
our ancestors buried deep within
their armors of resistance.

Let us stand tall in our privilege
and be proud of our choices,
when they had to surrender
to the swift tides of an ocean
that paid no heed to desire.

Let us be who we are
meant to be, unmasked,
unafraid, unmoored
by the expectations that
wore them down.

Let us be,
because they could not.

ACKNOWLEDGMENTS

This entire collection is a love letter to my immigrant parents, Arundhati and Debasis Chatterjee, who have truly sacrificed everything for our happiness. I do not know how you did it (and continue to do so), but I hope these poems show how much I appreciate and love you for *everything*.

To my brother, Pothik Chatterjee, you are truly the best gift and creative support system a sister could ask for. No one else believes me in the way you do, and your cover art is *chef's kiss.*

To my extraordinary daughter, Nainika, I also wrote this book for you. To understand the lives and legacies of all the women who came before you, and to tell you that *you are enough* just as you are. I love you.

To my husband, Suraj, and my darling son, Kavir, the most important men in my life. I am beyond grateful for your softness and your strength, and for your ability to lift me up every day.

To Rachel Clift, my incredible book designer and self-publishing coach, thank you for making me feel so safe and creatively empowered in your hands. To Freydis Lova, thank you for your thoughtful edits and kind words of encouragement.

To all my readers, from Instagram to *Desert Marigold* to *Vermilion Legacy*, you are the ones who give me the confidence to put my words out into the world. Thank you. Your voice matters.

And lastly to all the women who came before me— my mother, my grandmothers, my aunts, my great aunts, my ancestors. I feel your spirit guiding me every day. I hope I make you proud.

ABOUT THE AUTHOR

Godhuli Chatterjee Gupta is a first-generation South Asian American writer and poet. She is a former "third culture kid" who has grown up in six countries around the world and currently resides in the suburbs of Chicago raising her two children with her husband.

Godhuli attributes her love of poetry to her Bengali immigrant parents, who immersed her childhood with art, theater, film, and culture. Her colorful upbringing gives her a unique perspective on identity, language, borders, family, and relationships.

Godhuli has a bachelor's degree in Journalism and a master's degree in Integrated Marketing Communications from Northwestern University.

Her previous work includes the poetry collection *Desert Marigold.*

Website: wordsbygodhuli.com
Instagram: @wordsby.godhuli

Printed by Libri Plureos GmbH in Hamburg,
Germany

9 798234 036216